BRAVE COWARDS

Other books by David Mugun

"How to Undo Life's Airlocks." 2011

"10 Critical Success Answers for SMEs." 2012

"Rock Solid in All Seasons." 2017

Brave Cowards.

David Mugun

Published by

THE SCRIBE CENTRE

We are empowering the world

P.O.Box 35-00621, Nairobi, Kenya

First published 2018

3

Contents

DEDICATION

This is to the person eager to learn about life in the real world of employment.

ACKNOWLEDGEMENTS

To Almighty God for seeing me through with my 4th book.

To former colleagues who helped me in putting the script together. I owe you big time.

To all who have in one way or another aided in the writing of this book. I cannot list everyone by name but please accept my acknowledgment.

INTRODUCTION

This book is inspired by the need to motivate and mentor up-coming employees or businesspeople using real-life experiences.

Many people never open up to benefit others for various reasons. This book will not only dwell on what others did to me but, also where I went wrong and, what I would do now with hindsight.

It is only by giving the reader the full perspective, that he or she will appreciate the situations and learn from them.

Enjoy reading.

Chapter 1

A Story to set the pace.

Animals often give us something to learn from them. There was this famous animal orphanage that went out of its way to rescue abandoned or clearly endangered young animals found in the wild.

In this particular orphanage, a rhino calf was put in the same section with elephant calves for a number of years. The rhino grew up around elephants.

The town's development soon demanded a portion of this orphanage and authorities were forced to translocate the less endangered animals into the wild.

So the elephants and the rhino were freed at a point frequented by both species. Over time, the elephant calves integrated well with the dominant elephant herd in this park.

The rhino wondered between its own kind and the familiar elephants. Some elephants kept chasing it away. In the rhino's mind, it was just a game as was always the case at the orphanage.

To the elephants, it was serious business. It was about defending their territory and preserving the species. It was never the familiar ones that kept chasing the rhino; it was those that had been raised in the wild.

Those wild elephants appreciated the rhino as part of the ecosystem but never one of their own.

The message finally sunk when the patriarch jumbo, irked by the rhino's back and forth movements, inflicted deadly blows with its pointed tusks.

The naïve rhino finally limped away from the elephant herd for the last time.

In life, naivety is neither a logically understood and accepted shield for missing the point, nor is it the excusable position that warrants anyone a second chance at something.

The term "naïve rhino" shall be used repeatedly in the book to drive home the point.

Who are Brave-cowards?

The oxymoron "brave-cowards" adds to a list of special types of people whom when well -managed, makes life at the very least bearable or interesting and fruitful when they are fully contained.

It is easier to describe these types in plural because they come in a myriad of forms.

Brave-cowards mean people who are brave enough to break laws or rules in order to forestall perceived or real circumstances attributed to others from outpacing them.

They are cowardly because of their fear of competition and unwelcomed challenge. More precisely, it is an act of self-preservation or malicious efforts driven by the need to maintain the status quo at work or within a defined grouping.

When bravery is stirred by cowardly acts, innocent people suffer immensely or get disadvantaged. Doping in sports, acts of malice at work, deceitfulness in any aspect of life, all enliven the meaning of brave-cowards.

"It is me or no one else." Or "it must be me first then, others..." are the thoughts that occur in the heads of brave-cowards.

In this book, I use real-life examples of situations from my work- life, to aid readers to get a glimpse of the employment world and if already in employment, learn from mistakes or situations that I got into or found myself in.

Let me mention here that not every situation in this book will label those revealed as brave-cowards. Many of them, acted at the behest of, or the manipulation of brave-cowards.

Names will be altered to keep readers out of the potentially confrontational paths with those whom, they may suspect as the actual people in my work life.

I will also not mention the organizations by name but only by industry. Let me reveal here that at the time of writing this book, I had worked for a total of twenty-two years in nine organizations in the following industries.

 Office automation, Insurance, Banking, Business education and now my own consulting firm.

The experiences are actual, some ordinary and other surreal. The different industries that I have worked in, have aided in giving me a taste of the good and the ugly circumstances that are unique to those industries.

The one string that runs through all of them is the human element in all extremes.

I am forever grateful to all my past employers for they gave me work experiences that continue to resonate in my professional undertakings long after my departure.

Let me confirm, that these organizations that are a permanent feature in my resume' are all fine companies to work with and any unpleasant experiences encountered in my service to them, should not, and must not, be misconstrued as an indication of my thinking of them.

People never leave organizations, they run away from bosses and, the actions of individuals cannot be the actions of organizations.

Chapter 2

Working in the Office Automation Business.

Let me acknowledge that I gained my office discipline from a tea manufacturing company that I had been with for my university practicum and was now familiar with office etiquette. Several years later, they are my good client.

Shortly after completing my undergraduate degree program, I gained employment in the Office Automation industry. My first company sold photocopiers, faxes, computers, and the works.

It is here, that I was trained as a salesman and indeed tested my mettle by making some sales around the city of Nairobi. In a matter of months, I resigned to join my second employer.

My new employer was a better-structured outfit and was a subsidiary of a multinational. For a young employee, this was a godsend because training was frequent and incentives were far-reaching in my world then. The differences between my first and second employer were like night and day.

My new company had a better employee benefits structure, a fact attested to by the presence of many long-serving employees. A good number of colleagues were members of the Savings and Credit Cooperative – SACCO.

In those days, unsecured loans from banks were unheard of and hence SACCO membership was a necessity that was open to employees with a permanent staff status at this company.

I quickly settled to work because it was only a change of company in a familiar industry. Fast forward. This company had many events to either celebrate this, or, launch that, and better still, occasions to welcome new staff.

I was a straight shooter. Things were either black or white with nothing in between. Now I realize the true meaning and use of the word "tack", many people use "tact" to mean the same thing. I lacked tack.

My straight talking and quick nature off the blocks was not going down well with the veterans. Being young, confident and delivering targets, scared many people.

My monthly retainer was a decent sum of money but the now regular commissions made it even better and as if on a roll, more money triggered plenty of confidence to the extent that I felt as if I had been with this company for long.

On one sunny Saturday, we were invited to a SACCO meeting that would culminate in a feast of tasty food and fine drinks. This was the bait that I swallowed hook, line and sinker. As a young bachelor it was saving me money besides, it afforded me the opportunity to fraternize with the team.

The end of the meeting marked the beginning of the social bit. One drink kept introducing the next one into my system and soon, I was the life of the party. I was funny, impressive with my industry knowledge and in a mood to win over more friends.

I recall that we drifted to national politics and I paid glowing tribute to a budding politician who had in his first attempt, beaten a hitherto revered veteran. I went on to praise him for retaining his parliamentary seat in the recent elections after beating older and supposedly more experienced opponents.

As I went on, I noticed that everyone was unusually quiet, in fact, the kind of silence that tells you that, everyone else was eager for a new topic. That day ended well but we shall revisit it later.

As the months went by swiftly, my sales grow steadily. Very often, I had some money to throw the boys a round of drinks on Fridays and Saturdays.

At work, the sales team was divided into territories and product specializations.

My straight talk and political discussions had kicked off a storm that was kept away from me for a while. A colleague had been quietly eyeing my portfolio of customers and had also realized that my approved products sales mandate delivered more money in sales commissions than those he earned from his product specialization mandate. We were selling different products and mine were of higher value.

This colleague had a penchant for backstabbing whilst keeping close to conceal his deadly intentions. Armed with a plan to dislodge me and, motivated by the office mummers about me; he set the ball rolling.

My colleague's plan coincided with two events. The first was, getting my immediate boss to believe that I was snooping on him on behalf of Kenya Revenue Authority -KRA. Unknown to me, my boss had a side hustle. KRA had just been reenergized to collect taxes and anyone in business at the time was fearful of the stated consequences of evasion.

My boss was made to believe that I was the enemy within, and he wasted no time in letting me know that my days were numbered at this company.

As I wondered at where my boss was coming from with the accusations, the Marketing Manager who was much higher in rank than my immediate boss introduced a sales incentive. This marked the second event that I had mentioned in the previous paragraph.

We were approaching the year-end, and the marketing budget still had some money to motivate the sales numbers so that, the attainment of targets would result in handsome bonuses.

A competition running the whole month was introduced to reward the top salesperson weekly.

The reward was thirty thousand shillings a week for the person who sold the most boxes or the highest value boxes or both in the event of a tie. "Boxes" was the term used for machines as they came in boxes. In 1996, thirty thousand shillings was plenty of money.

In the first week of the competition, nobody won. In the second week, a lady colleague won and was given her money at the weekly meeting. This got everyone on overdrive.

In the third week, a male colleague won and got paid. All of us were reminded that the last week was now ticking away and that it was now or never.

I did all that I could possibly do because I not only needed the money but a win would go a long way to dissuade my boss from frustrating me. It would move me from a liability to an asset, so I thought!

The list on the wall was updated after 5 PM and on Monday; I was not on the list. Tuesday, a small copier got my name up but not enough to threaten anyone.

On Wednesday, a larger copier took me to position three and on Thursday, nothing changed.

On Friday afternoon, I received a call from a prospective customer who had been on my radar screen and progressively getting hotter over a three month period.

I went over to his offices and he handed me a purchase order for two copiers and a full payment by cheque. It was now 4:30 PM and my ride back to the office was agonizingly slowed down by the Friday traffic jams.

The driver tried everything that he could possibly do to get me to the office in time. This was "landline Kenya" where cell phones were restricted to the powerful few and no communication with the office was possible to save the day so far.

At 4:55 PM, I strolled into the office calm and collected. The rest of the team had congregated at the noticeboard and celebrations had started. I had been written-off at this point.

I reached into my folder and pulled out the purchase order and everyone shouted: "it does not count till full payment is made." I then pulled out the cheque and because it was from a reputable firm, it counted.

It now was a switch by those in celebration into the mute mode and the silent set of colleagues erupting in my support. I had beaten them hands down.

This win elicited mixed emotions. Some people openly told me that they would see to it that I never got paid and that the person, who came a distant second, would be paid.

The weekly meetings took place on Tuesdays. On Monday morning, I reached the office very early and unusually found the Human Resources Manager –HRM spiritedly pacing up and down around my seating area.

He immediately summoned me into his office and handed me a brown envelop and accompanied it with the words, "you failed to fit in." He then said to me, "this is your termination letter but you can save face by resigning so that we can consider your benefits".

With youthful courage on my side, I knew that I would land myself another job. What occupied me at the time was the thirty thousand bob due to me from the just concluded competition.

As word went round that I had been terminated from employment, the mean colleagues shouted at me "we told you that you will not get paid".

I eventually got paid for the win and all outstanding money due to me but, I had to sign a clearance form that indicated that by signing, I had nothing against the organization.

So what happened exactly? Here you are performing your duties diligently and exceeding your sales targets yet, you are out of a job!

A sympathetic colleague invited me for a cup of tea at a restaurant some meters away from the office. After expressing sorrow at my situation, he took me back to the day of the SACCO meeting.

The political discussion that I had so enthusiastically initiated became my undoing. Remember everyone in the room went silent.

It so happens that the veteran politician was the father of the Human Resources Manager. The same manager had tried his hand in politics more recently and was beaten by the young politician that I had fondly talked about.

Both father and son had been beaten by my preferred candidate albeit in two different elections. A special arrangement had allowed the HRM back to his post at the office.

At the SACCO meeting, I walked myself into a landmine by unnecessarily annoying the HRM.

This then gained traction with the old guard because of my straight talk and the frequent teasing by the Marketing Manager who kept quipping "why are you allowing a rookie salesman to beat you guys". My presence was unsettling for the old guard.

The colleague, who wanted my job so badly, got my boss into the fray just to complete the set of powerful enemies around me.

On my way to say my goodbyes to the CEO of English descent, an overjoyed mate in sales shouted: "if you were from our community, we would have solved this thing quietly". He finished off by saying to me "you go to that Member of Parliament whom you praise so much, to save you!"

The CEO was short in his remarks. "I give my managers the space to make decisions and clearly, you are one of our finest commercially but, you got on someone's rough edge".

Can this experience happen today in Kenya? Yes!

So, how did I go wrong?

The term "due diligence" is often used in the corporate world around the time one is intending to take over an organization or is checking out the suitability and compatibility of a potential business partner. One would usually have a tick list and a methodology for undertaking the exercise. On my part, my tick list must have been too basic.

First, I never undertook what again in the corporate world is referred to as "environmental scanning" or ecosystem scan".

I needed to have known better of the intricacies that held together the relationships in the close-knit office family. I became the naïve rhino and young or not, there was no mercy.

The execution was ruthless, fast and furious so that the territory was protected and their "species" was preserved.

I now realize that doing well at work is no license to cause the discomfort of others. When you are competing for any scarce resource, conflict is the inevitable result. What varies is the intensity. The scarce resource here was the recognition for excellent work.

The older guys never took the Marketing Manager's comments lightly whenever he used my performance to tease them into positive action. He ignited lethal action in them.

I caused the HRM grief by embarrassing him about his failure to clinch the parliamentary seat. By challenging the oldies, I handed him a ready stream of allies' hell-bent on sorting me out.

I caused the colleague who sold "lesser" products to get jealous of my position. This triggered in him the desire to see me out of the way and when it happened, he was rewarded with my territory and portfolio and of cause he went ahead to earn commissions for my efforts! I lost out big time.

I also over-relied on personal competence to keep me on the job. You see, when everyone on the team is good at their job, other attributes become the differentiators.

The boss can think to himself that if "I did away with this guy, I can still make budget by year-end". All he has to do is to push the remaining guys a bit harder and then onboard a new person.

Staying employed is also an interpersonal relationship duty. There is a belief that in the corporate world, there is no forgiving, therefore, you must work in ways that don't leave behind unnecessary residual bad feelings towards you.

There are cases of people falling out of favour with one another, and as a result, one of them leaves for another organization. The other colleague over time then joins the same company.

Their toxic history from the previous company may as it has happened to many, erupt with deadly consequences. It is only mountains that never meet.

Let me also add that the word "friendly" is not a euphemism for the word "confidant". At the workplace, people get friendly for their own reasons but the naïve rhino may take them for friends. Play along without giving in to their dalliance.

Finally, find a way of being professionally close to your boss. In my case, I realized this when it was too late, that my boss was closer to the other colleagues despite my delivering for him on the commercial front.

If I had kept a close relationship with him, then he would have first confirmed the allegations around the KRA with me, or better still, he would have doubted them.

Chapter 3

Back in the Industry.

It never took long before I was back in the industry. The company that I joined had a presence in the other East African Community countries. Unlike my previous employer, this company was run by the owners. Decisions were instant and had no time zone challenges.

Having fully nursed the wounds inflicted on me previously, I was keen to grow and improve my capabilities. I recall that my first few months felt like walking on eggs. I was very careful and took my time to learn about everything that I needed to know.

I knew the industry well but I never openly demonstrated it to anyone lest I got flailed in the wake of their wrath.

As is the case with everything in life, the bosses were businesslike but some people within the administrative chain cared less about anyone but themselves. Whenever you crossed someone's path, it was discussed in informal forums.

One such forum was the cook-out forum famously referred to as "*koroga*" a Swahili word meaning to mix, and in this instance, the action of mixing the chili filled fried chicken or mutton. Men would agree on when and where to have the *koroga* on Fridays or Saturdays.

Attendance was strictly by invitation and if bad vibes about you made it to the discussions, it was unlikely that you would ever get invited. The camaraderie around the *koroga* boys was evident and no one dared to cross their path.

I enjoyed my work at this company and got to make good contacts. The traveling was good. I recall making a big sale to a leading hotel chain that had game lodges in Samburu, Maasai Mara, and Amboseli national parks.

I delivered machines to all their lodges and hotels in Nairobi and Mombasa and got free game drives at the lodges and extra days in Mombasa.

My experiences in these places never made it to the office discussions because the *koroga* boys would protest at why it was not assigned to one of them.

This company participated in many technology type exhibitions that got us exposed to many decision makers. We closed many sales from such forums but we never credited most of the sales to the exhibitions because the *koroga* gang was ready to label us as "only good after exhibitions".

The other good part of this company was the sponsorship of the various motor rallies. The company would donate computers and copiers for use at the check-points and obviously, they had to be manned.

This afforded us a much sought after cash allowance and, a day out watching man, machine, and terrain attempting to outsmart the other to much applause and, merrymaking.

With improved interpersonal skills, I gained the acceptance of the *koroga* boys and I got to learn a lot about what was happening in the company. One of the initiatives soon in the offing was the planned entry into the PVC cards and machines business.

In the late nineties, this was an innovative idea. There was much promise. The market was untapped. So when everyone was scared of being moved to start this new department, I saw a huge opportunity.

I moved to a new seating area and got assigned to a new boss. The *koroga* boys put in a good word and we hit it off on a high note.

I had to quickly learn the markets, the competition and the path of least resistance to making successful sales.

The product applications were many, banks purchased the machines to make their own ATM cards, Medical insurance companies needed them to make photo-based medical cards. Microchip technology was new and the machines had this capability too.

There was a huge potential in the government market. The military needed good cards, the police and institutions of higher learning were in our sights.

Once I settled into my new role, big things began to happen for me. The machine manufacturers sent me ideas on where else to sell the machines and provided me with comparisons of such uses in more advanced countries.

One that caught my enthusiasm was that of using the PVC card on firearms license. In those days, the police section responsible for firearms licensing was located at the present day traffic department off Ngong road.

I went to see a Senior Police officer. He listened to me attentively and displayed all the buying signals that a salesman prays to pick out in a sales pitch. My enthusiasm resonated well with him and then, the policeman in him took over.

"Young man, where do you come from?" "How long have you been in this business?" As I kept answering, he kept asking more and more. It felt like an interrogation but he was just being who he was, a good policeman.

He then said to me "Please listen very carefully because I usually don't have time for salesmen." "Since you have demonstrated respect, I will help you out."

He then went on to explain to me that as much as he wanted to adapt the PVC technology because it was tamperproof when compared to the paper type in use, his hands were tied.

He made me understand that all government documents were defined in the acts of parliament that give them legality. His advice was that we focus on lobbying Members of Parliament – MPs to amend the clauses relating to firearms licensing documentation.

The senior Policeman also wished me luck in this endeavor because printing was monopolized by the government printer and any spillover at the time, favored companies where the same MPs had interests.

For my company, this was very good market development feedback. As we pursued this effort, I had to meet my targets. So I kept all energies in tandem as a one-man show because my boss was focused on other pressing matters.

I managed to get to know and meet a powerful member of the relevant committee of parliament. We got talking and I explained the reasons behind my mission.

His role as an Assistant cabinet minister was going to be of much help as he was part of the system.

My expectations were for him to champion the same with his colleagues. We had several meetings but each one of them only served to make his intentions of competing with my employers, clearer.

He wanted to set up his own company, then, push parliament into amending the acts to suit the technology and the applications that I was selling. This man was fascinating and could get you to say yes when you never meant to.

I came face to face with conflict of interest. I had introduced a business possibility to an MP who now wanted both the idea and my services to consummate his newly acquired ambitions.

A quick check with his other business interests showed me that he was a bad employer. The employee turnover was very high and I could easily become a statistic very quickly.

When he sensed my reluctance to join him, he threatened to tell my employer that I was forcing him to employ me.

Here I was, a young powerless man facing a formidable MP endowed with the gift of the gab, resources to intimidate me and a privileged minister's position to boot. I was again the naïve rhino in the midst of marauding elephants.

The MP said to me, "let me make it easy and quick, I will tell your boss that you are bothering me for a job instead of lobbying for the much-needed changes in the firearms act."

I was in a catch 22 situation. I could not take my enthusiasm off the lobbying efforts and, I did not want to annoy the MP. So I asked for time to think about the offer. Lucky for me, we had no mobile phones in those days and for some reason, the MP always called my office when I was out in the field.

I suggested to my boss, that it was better for us if he took over the lobbying efforts because I was feeling the strain on my targets. I could not achieve them if I had to spend time with the MP besides; my boss was a member of many prestigious clubs that were suitable for such meetings.

I also told my boss to keep it at the back of his mind that the MP was thinking of plunging into our business space through a new outfit. My boss was very appreciative of this information and took over the lobbying efforts.

As fate had it, I knew that I was now safe when I heard on the lunchtime news bulletin that the MP had been relieved of his ministerial duties by the president for undisclosed reasons. He may have messed with someone else. With this sacking, the MP went into political hibernation.

I parted myself on the back for not messing up and rewarded myself with a drink after 5 PM. I sipped in celebration and was happy that I was finally out of harm's way and dalliance with a brave-coward.

As this episode was ending, another one was brewing. I got a call from the Africa Representative of the card machines company. They wanted me to fly down south for training. Every time they took it up with my immediate boss, something seemed to happen. My boss was against the idea. It had come up for discussion at the last *koroga* and, no wonder I was not invited.

To the *koroga* boys, it had never happened that a Kenyan of African origin had benefited from training abroad. Behind the scenes, schemes were in motion to get one of them to go for this training. The Africa Representative resisted any other name.

I had another complication. My passport had expired and in those years, it could take up to three months to have it renewed yet, the trip was in a week's time.

I talked to my Dad and he asked me to travel from Nairobi to our home in the Rift Valley. The next day, he drove me to the Kisumu immigration office where he had good contacts. The passport was renewed the same day and I was back in Nairobi with a brand new passport much to the bewilderment of my unsupportive boss.

I encountered another bottleneck. The South African government had just imposed visa requirements on Kenyans. Previously you just booked a ticket and boarded a plane headed down south.

The lead time was a week but I was now well within four days of travel and I pleaded for consideration at the embassy. I was advised to leave my passport with them and be prepared for any eventuality.

As we awaited the visa news, my boss went ahead to assign me duties for the week that I would hopefully be away. It was a foregone conclusion in his mind that I would not travel. So I grudgingly took the instructions and started making calls to the customers that I had been assigned.

In the midst of my sorrows, a call came through from the embassy asking me to pick my passport. Thank God! I had a visa. I went straight away to the finance manager to process my overseas allowance. For some reason, he was in a good mood that afternoon.

He asked his team to process the allowance and then, to obtain my boss's signature, more as a formality.

On the day I said my goodbyes for the week to my immediate boss, I had the director's blessings and allowances in my pocket.

In those days, traveling down south was a big deal. In fact, most ladies in the office sent me to buy for them a pair of shoes that was trending at the time. I recall making a handsome profit from these shoes.

Having encountered the wrath of brave-cowards in my previous company, I was not about to open up myself to more abuse and punishment in this company. I worked well till I moved on to another industry.

Chapter 4

Joining the Insurance Industry

After one of the incidences between the *koroga* boys and myself, I vowed to move on to another company. I attended interviews in earnest and the rewards were painfully slow.

One afternoon, the phone rang and on picking it, a pleasant voice invited me to a job interview with an insurance company.

A week down the road, I was seated in the reception area awaiting my turn. I had my best shoes on alongside my favorite suit and a shirt and matching tie.

I walked into the interview room and met the Marketing Manager and five Branch Managers. It was while in there that I got to know what position I was interviewing for. The company needed a number of Unit Managers. These were to report to the Branch Managers.

I had a good forty-five minutes in there and when I walked out, I had a good feeling. Three months went by and I knew that I missed out on the job.

One afternoon, the same voice that had invited me for the interview, asked me on phone to go over and meet with the Marketing Manager.

The Marketing Manager was clear about having filled in all the Unit Manager positions and momentarily I felt wasted. Then he said to me. I want you to be my Assistant Marketing Manager. It turned out that all the branch managers in the panel had wanted me on their teams.

Assistant Marketing Manager was senior to Unit Manager and this was very exciting for me.

I was invited for another interview with the General Manager overseeing the division and a final one with the Managing Director.

With my letter in the pocket, I immediately tendered my resignation and gave a month's notice. As the news spread in the organization, the *koroga* boys invited me to the next cook-out that Friday.

Every one of them pleaded with me not to leave. Promises of salary increases filled the air and so did the more appealing spices used to cook the chicken that evening.

At the end of it all, I never burned bridges. We continued attending motor rallies and *korogas*.

My first day at work in the insurance industry was an interesting one. I was assigned a manager's desk and the trappings of the office. A sense of arrival into the next level invaded my thoughts.

The next day, I was shipped off to the industrial area branch for a week to familiarize myself with branch operations.

In week two, I was taken around head office operations and at the end of the month, I wrote and handed in a report to my boss. One of the things that I did early enough was to win his trust and soon, he copied me in on most of the things in the department.

I quietly found out that all managers had to undergo a six months' probation and then got confirmed on successful completion thereafter. My letter read three months. I decided to work hard and smart then, confront the HRM for my confirmation in three months' time.

In my second month, the branch manager in Eldoret resigned and I was asked to go in to act. I found a dispirited branch operating from a dubious location because the building housing it previously, had just gone up in flames.

The other insurance companies were taking away customers at will and it did not help things that, one of the insurance companies in town had just collapsed.

It was a fearful time to be in the insurance industry. Our competitors only needed to remind our customers of our poor location and told customers to be careful about a company that could not even afford good premises. So on optics alone, we were losing out badly.

So, my first task was to work in haste with the property manager at the head office, and the contractor on the ground to finish off the works, and move the team to the well-spruced space. We moved and then worked on the team members' self-belief. The reset button worked magic.

My Marketing Manager supported my efforts and we financed and sent teams out to the markets around. We introduced incentives and we spent time in the field.

You know that all other products are bought. Insurance is the only one that must be sold to make money. We did so and turned the tide.

My stay in the branch was only for three months during which time I had identified potential Branch Manager Job candidates who were interviewed and thereafter, I handed over to the successful candidate.

The return to my duties in Nairobi was short lived. I was sent to Machakos to set up a new branch. I swept the office on the first day and then went ahead to hire office staff and then the sales agents and Unit Managers. My good work in Eldoret had been noted because the branch was now exceeding its targets.

I realized that I needed to seize the moment because I could not predict how Machakos would turn out. My first three months had been successful. At my young age, my social ratings would hit the roof if I had a car. There were enough motivations to seize the moment.

So I went out to look for a car, filled in the forms and submitted them through the system. Shortly thereafter, I got a call from the HR manager asking me to see him. He shot straight to the point. "You have three more months to first get confirmed, and secondly, then to qualify for a car loan."

I reluctantly reached my coat pocket and pulled out my appointment letter. I brought out the three months' probation period to his attention and the fact that the Managing Director had signed the letter.

A meeting between the HRM and the Marketing Manager was arranged to deliberate this unprecedented three months instead of six months bottleneck. The numbers were on my side, I had turned around a branch and now I had been handed a new one. Management needed to demonstrate to the board that entry to Machakos was a good decision.

Eventually, I was confirmed and my car loan was approved. For the next fourteen months, I built the branch but remained the official Assistant Marketing Manager as I was keen to operate from Nairobi.

I had no trouble with my Marketing Manager. There was beef with some fellows in the Finance department. Twice while in Eldoret and severally in Machakos, my salary kept being "forgotten" at end month. When I could take it no more, I reported for work at the head office and went to occupy my desk as Assistant Marketing Manager.

Initially, my boss thought that I was finishing off some work but then he realized that I was around after lunch. He asked me why I was not in Machakos and I Informed of my predicament.

I actually requested him to ask anyone of his choice from the finance department to travel down to the branch in my place as I could not afford to go down.

In the meantime, I had found work to do from the Head office. So technically, I was working as per my appointment letter and therefore no disciplinary action could be preferred on me.

My boss hit the roof and armed with evidence of a recurrence over several months, the Finance honchos had no defense. I had to get paid the same day.

My complaints about salary payments triggered a totally unrelated branch audit. When someone is looking for you, they will find you and the first audit cleared the branch management. It was just a warning.

Soon thereafter, I noticed suspicious behavior in the office, the secretary, the messenger and the clerk kept walking out. I shut the door and quickly followed them and at a distance, I heard them wondering aloud how they would cover the shortage. Shortage!? I asked myself.

I called the clerk aside and he told me that the petty cash was missing. It may have sounded like a small matter but not anymore when finance department boys are out for your skull.

I immediately informed my boss and reached out to the branch accountant at head office. The matter was well handled but not without branch staff spending a night at the police cells.

This incident awoke some people at the head office. On the surface, people are colleagues but deeper inside, one of my staffers, was a close relative of a senior manager. The handling of the cash loss case irked him so much so that he found cheer and camaraderie from a specific guy working in the finance department.

He blamed me for what had befallen his relative in Machakos. The branch mail started missing this item or, the other and, another audit was ordered.

This time around I had someone from the big office after me and collaborators in my branch helping out. Since I strictly never ever handled any cash directly, it was hard to pin me down with lost money.

Since the branch was exceeding its commercial targets, it was hard to pin me down on this front.

So the plan was to demonstrate that I was a weak administrator. To this end, an audit was called to check on everything in the branch. So all assets were checked against the assets register and all was well. A branch does not have too many things but this audit lasted a whole day and nothing was found to be out of order.

At the end of it all, the idea was to get the office staff to complain about me so that my confirmation could not happen. All along, the finance guys believed that my car loan approval was because of my special working circumstances as a roving manager who got sent out to fix branches.

From discussions with other colleagues, it became clear to me that some new staff had had their confirmations delayed or declined because of complaints from other departments.

Much as my branch was performing, I had learned that performance alone is not enough to keep you at work. Had I gone with the expected six months' probation period, I perhaps would never have been confirmed regardless of good commercial performance.

There were strong rumors that someone in the Finance department, went to the Managing Director's office to highlight the contents of my appointment letter.

The MD was in the picture and he simply asked this finance department staffer "who signed the letter?" to which he answered "you sir" and he was asked to explain the problem to which he said that, he was doing it for audit purposes. That was a smart exit.

Much as it never came up again, the truth of the matter is that my appointment letter was written, alongside those of some junior staff who were employed with me, at the same time.

The person who typed out the appointment letter wrote it over the earlier letter and, really only changed my name and title and took it in for signature.

I stayed on to enjoy my job at this company and left a mark that got noticed in the industry and hence my next move. I had encountered and successfully managed some brave-cowards.

I still respect my boss to this day because he stood by me all along.

This particular insurance company was the cradle of many of my passions today. My interest in Human Resources work was nurtured here.

When you deal with salespeople, you run a parallel effort from the organization's human resources department in recruiting, training, supervising and motivating salespeople.

The development of training material for the business team alongside those of branch support staff fell into my area of responsibility.

When you can to a great degree of precision, handle Sales and Marketing matters, and once you can in tandem run with day-to-day Human Resources affairs, and can set up branches and get them to break even quickly; everyone takes note.

These abilities resonated well with the executive management and being a newcomer to the industry, they did not bode well with some people in the organization and, particularly those who felt that I was too young.

I will admit that I too had this chip on the shoulder that never helped things at all times. I recall one day getting into an unnecessary fight with an office veteran at the head office.

This lady had been with the company for years, in fact, when she joined this insurance firm, I was still in primary school. But here I was, a manager and there she was, working as part of the underwriting back office team.

On that day, my branch team had complained about the turnaround time taken by the underwriting department, to get policy documents out.

This was affecting our chances of closing more business with new customers because; their colleagues would dissuade them from signing up till their policy documents were delivered to them.

When my pleas to catch the attention of the lady in question, proved futile, my patience soon turned into anger. This lady made remarks to the effect that she was not employed to handle the issues of one branch but all others and, that I should be respectful to my elders.

She uttered a few more slurs to which I protested "this is not a village where age reins over all else, it is an office where seniority is based on rank and not age alone."

Since the scene of the action was at an open plan office set up, everyone's attention was drawn to the fight. It became a tussle between the young and the old and soon pleas for a sense of calm and professional conduct were made to quell the deteriorating situation.

When peace finally prevailed, none of us cared to apologize to the other and to avert a further incident, it was agreed that another underwriting colleague, would henceforth handle my branch's policy documents.

This fight kept the lady and me away from each other's paths until the day of the end-of-year staff party. I approached her and said to her, "my elder, It was a tough year but please let bygones be bygones. Please forgive me."

In jest, she replied, "my son, in village language and senior in the office, I forgive you." We tossed to our new found truce and agreed to work well together moving forward.

Let me just add that, when you are young and working in the midst of older colleagues, please care to empathize with them.

Many people do not take lightly to the challenges paused by vibrant and firebrand youngsters, who never take the time to acquaint themselves, with varying personalities at work.

On that note, I easily was the brave-coward in this particular incident save for the fact that I was helping out with customer service for my branch and not self preservation.

Chapter 5

The Second Insurance Company.

One afternoon, in the year 2001, I received a phone call from a former colleague. This gentleman had worked with me previously at my first insurance company.

My first insurance company had proved to be a good hunting ground for good employees. About four other colleagues from the branches had crossed over to the company now courting me.

I was invited to interview with them and underwent a rigorous process and eventually emerged successful. For my first three months, I was assigned to head a branch.

Things soon changed and, I was assigned responsibility for six branches. Four were fully established and two were to be set up from scratch. My previous experience came to the fore as I found myself in familiar territory in so far as new branches set up were concerned.

The unfamiliar side was equally interesting. Besides having a branch in Nairobi, the rest were spread far apart with three of them triangulating Mt. Kenya. Thika and Machakos were to commence shortly.

My new bosses were seconded from a parent company in South Africa. The work style was quite different from all others that I had been a part of. Decisions were made quickly and the speed of execution was also fast-paced.

To remain in the good books of these bosses, one had to follow through on all agreed action items. I wasted no time in proving my mettle and soon found out that my balance gravitated around execution, quality reporting and maintaining a good working relationship with my bosses.

The flipside of this approach was that whereas it delighted the bosses by guaranteeing results, the tactics did little to inspire the cooperation of many other teammates in support roles.

With hindsight, when one is taken through a baptism by fire on account of high expectations, in an environment that has quick decision makers, you are forced to focus on the core areas of responsibility.

Many instances of friction with coworkers were the order of the day. This was a high-pressure environment.

It was very likely for any one of your direct reports to get lined up to take over from you right under your nose. The worst experience would be where those below you were working hard to get you out of the way with the aid of senior managers.

Before I narrate a memorable experience, I will credit this company for inculcating in me a number of skills that remain dear to me. My scribe love came from writing board papers for my boss.

Everything had to make sense and I had to find the correct words to transfer the purposed meaning to whoever read the papers. This experience planted in me the ability to write fast and also the need to produce well-researched papers.

At the national stage, we were witnessing transition politics at play. The President that we had had for twenty-four years was stepping down at the end of his constitutional mandate. It was a significant moment because it had never happened before in Kenya.

The political atmosphere found its way into the company but the foreign bosses could not pick the undertones that were rather obvious to the rest of us and at times, it was possible to find one selected against by the tide.

This is where my bachelorhood ended and that is where the next paragraph finds its bearing.

As the country was headed to a general election, I took leave to get married.

While on leave, I got invited for lunch by my boss at a restaurant near to company headquarters in town. The bosses had indicated that since they would be away for the Christmas holidays during the wedding ceremony, they wanted us to have lunch.

I found my bosses from South Africa in the company of my colleagues in the commercial department. It looked strange but I settled down to the sumptuous lunch and washed it down with a glass of wine.

Then the big boss informed me of what was happening at my branch in Nyeri. "Your in-laws are misbehaving." Then he clarified that he meant the Nyeri branch. It was clear to me that there was a discussion around the table before my arrival.

The Nyeri branch was on a go-slow because, as the most prolific branch at the time, the sales numbers plummeted to levels never seen before that particular week. They were way behind the new branches and it concerned everyone.

51

So I was given instructions to drive down to the branch despite being on leave with a stern message. I was also instructed to put everyone on what in today's lingo is the equivalent of a Performance Improvement Plan-PIP. Whenever one was put on such a plan, their days were numbered if no significant improvement followed.

It is one of those situations that you are condemned if you do it or not. The reaction was furious. All but one person from the branch never honored my wedding invitation. All other branches that worked with me had a good representation.

The only person, who attended the wedding from this branch, had offered his car as part of the wedding convoy and decided to keep his word. I remain thankful to him.

Threats of resignations by the most prolific and old agents were noted at the headquarters. I was summoned by the General Manager who was acting as CEO at the time.

He looked ready to terminate my contract because he could not fathom how someone on leave could show up at a branch and commit the kind of things that I had just done.

I explained myself out and he decided to leave the matter pending till the CEO returned.

Soon after my wedding, we went to the general elections. A new president was elected. Kenyans were rated at the time as the most optimistic people in the world. It was a new dawn. For my Nyeri branch, one thing was clear, they were from the new President's home turf and wanted to be as happy as the other Kenyans.

My visit had brought untold humiliation and they sought an audience with the CEO. The CEO asked me to accompany him. We set out very early in the morning and the CEO kept asking me if I had a solution to the problem at the branch.

When he asked me again about my game plan, I knew that I was in trouble alone. It did not matter that a few weeks earlier, they had summoned me from my leave with express instructions.

Let me walk you through the unfolding situation in slow motion.

Seeing that I was alone in the matter, and in light of the new developments in the country, I was aware, that the team could demand my removal. This was a possibility because thus far, no one had admitted to sending me to the branch earlier.

It was increasingly clear, that a number of people wanted the unfolding situation to overwhelm me.

Here I am newly married and need the job more than ever before.

At that moment, I received a text message from a senior manager in the know of things. As he wished me luck, he wrote a shocking revelation. The unfolding drama right from my wedding boycott to what I went to resolve that morning had been anticipated by a senior manager high up the ladder.

At that moment, I had no game plan and began to resign to my fate.

Not even the overall sales target attainment by my cluster of six branches at the end of the year, as a matter of fact, could save me.

It felt like I had been thrown under the bus and now just waiting to be run over.

As we alighted from our now safely parked car, some cheeky agents shouted, "I wish this guy can be urgently released to go and work for the Moi Foundation." in reference to the newly retired president's chosen vehicle for public service engagements.

We got into the meeting room just to ensure that where the CEO sat was proper. I excused myself to use the washroom though I had no urge for it.

I said a little prayer. "God, if this is it, please give me the strength to overcome the loss of my job and if not, please give me something to say, so that this matter is resolved as You know, I was only obeying my boss; In Jesus name, I pray, Amen."

I then walked back into the meeting room and immediately felt the thickness of the tension in the room.

What I did next, was not in my plans. I felt in me a renewed sense of confidence and words began to flow in a logical sequence.

I asked the forty member-strong branch team to choose five representatives to articulate their grievances.The rest of them were to leave for the field for it was a workday.

The plan now was to let the CEO and I walk out of the room for fifteen minutes so that the whole team could put together their issues.

When we walked back into the room, the rest of the team walked out and we were left with five representatives together with the Branch Manager.

We tackled every point raised and got a commitment from them never to stage another go-slow. My boss was not expecting the positive turn of events.

We terminated the services of those who showed no progress and quickly got things back to business as usual.

This approach, proved effective because it forced the agents to prioritize the important things. It left the cheeky lot and the poor performers exposed because we deprived them of the "safety in numbers" advantage, a much sought-after ingredient when setting the stage for a chaotic meeting.

Those hell-bent on a drama-filled morning were swiftly dealt with by the five able representatives, who were obviously high up in the pecking order of branch matters.

Most of the hecklers in the team were working in cahoots with head office conspirators who pulled the strings from a distance. I had warded off the efforts of tireless brave-cowards who had infiltrated one of my branches.

On the way back, the CEO kept mentioning how well everything had gone. Deep down, I could see the hands of some senior managers in the problems of the branch.

Shortly after this, I noticed that I was assigned several ad hoc duties and assignments besides my regular work. Many times, I found my weekends lost to office work.

I recall that in that particular year, I missed watching the Rugby Safari Sevens tournament because I worked throughout the weekend to complete some work. This was painful but the work was termed "excellent" by the bosses.

The extra assignment was made urgent and made to coincide with the sevens tournament because, everyone then, knew how passionate I was about rugby matters. During the weekly Tuesday meeting, two guys sarcastically asked: "so how did it go at the sevens?" Their cheeky smiles sold them out.

I told them, I enjoyed it very much and that I loved the high quality of the event that year. One of them then asked, "You mean that you actually attended it?" "What will you report on today seeing that it needed a whole weekend to put together?"

It became clear, that when they could not fault me through the branch network, the group against me found ways to get me assigned more work so that I could give up. I chose to look at the bright side of things and accepted the additional work as good experience.

In conversations with former workmates at this company, they revealed to me that many conspirators in the ranks were frustrated by my attitude to embrace the extra work that came my way.

It had been debated in some circles that I would crumble and in the process, the quick decision making guys from South Africa would dismiss me. This never happened.

There was also a well-orchestrated move between some branch staff, headquarters staff and someone in the IT department, to leak out my email messages so that they all knew what I was up to. I stumbled upon this by accident while on a branch visit.

I was at a branch and I needed to refer to a document that I had sent out a month earlier. So as we scrolled through the branch manager's mailbox, we came across messages meant for senior management and in some cases responses to people outside the organization. I was shocked and angry.

The branch manager felt embarrassed that I now knew that he was part of the many recipients of unintended mail.

I talked to one of the IT department staff and soon discovered that this was a well-crafted conspiracy. When I uncovered the masterminds, the list had several silent killers hitherto "friendly and helpful". The surveillance was not restricted to me alone but was extended to six others.

The guys who looked the most approachable were part of the scheme and when word went round that I had decoded the schemers, every one of them found a convenient way of reaching out to me to blame the others.

When you gain access to information that you are otherwise not meant to have, you clearly have privileged information. Such information is not admissible as evidence in a court of law because it was obtained illegally. Brave-cowardice is about breaking rules and laws for self-preservation.

The idea behind the regular leaking of my email messages was to humiliate me if I discovered it, and also to get ahead of me on any plans that I had.

This was my first encounter with cyber-related war. As a rule of thumb, never ever think that all is well all the time at work. Have the allowance in your mind for time to retrace or review your steps. If you do not inspect, then do not expect.

Chapter 6

The Third Insurance Company

My quest to earn more whilst caring for my young family caught on, just as it would anybody. The room for advancement and the opportunity to apply my experience made this third insurance company attractive.

I went through a long process initiated by a headhunter and culminated in a final interview with the Managing Director.

My job was cut out. A Marketing Manager tasked with setting up a whole life operation from nearly scratch. It involved the development of products and a sales team on one hand and, systems and processes, on the other hand, a tall order for anyone in the business.

There existed a little group life business activity that piggy-backed on a very successful general insurance business side.

My efforts later on, contributed to the separation of the Life insurance business into a fully-fledged Life Insurance company.

My work-life in this company was under a composite model where the Life and General operations reported to one Managing Director.

By now, I was well versed with the entire business operational setup and knew where to start and what to do next. In total, I set up four branches spread around the country. One in Kisumu and Mombasa, and two in Nairobi.

We developed several products and had them successfully launched into the competitive market.

From a situation of no agents at all, I recruited 150 of them by the time that I left the organization. I had five of my agents qualify for the national agents' awards within our first full year of operation. Many more qualified in the succeeding years. This was no mean feat.

We had very intense strategic planning sessions annually that were followed up by quarterly review sessions attended by the MD and all the managers.

I never ever had a problem with the executive management as they were supportive at all times. At that time, the Chairman of the company was very supportive of the business and had a penchant for challenging newly employed managers. He wanted to rest assured that the company had the right team on board. Once he was sure that you were up to the task, he left you to go about with your job.

Often most of us who were new managers, would avoid coming face-to-face with him in the early days. He had a sharp mind that was ready to fault or support you in equal measure. Speaking to him amounted to facing a moment of truth.

One early morning, I drove in passed the Chairman's parking and round the building to my slot. The chairman was alighting from his car at the time. I took a few minutes in the car so that the chairman would have taken the lift by the time I reached it to go up to my workstation.

I was shocked to find him. He said, "let us go up, I was waiting for you." He had learned our tricks. We then went to his office and he took out a notepad, wrote my name at the top and proceeded to ask me a myriad of questions. He took notes as we talked. He agreed with many of my answers but disagreed with some.

As time went by, we came to have a good relationship and when other new managers joined the team, it was their turn to face the chairman. He did this without interfering with the executive management's mandate. I admired that focus from the top. In fact, none of my problems were with the board level people. They were all at the levels below them.

Upon joining the company, I was quick off the blocks. I got on my team a special kind of agent the kind that every team wishes to have. This lady, joined my team, underwent training and proceeded to the field and made good sales in her first week.

Within two months of joining us, her regular commissions were upwards of 150K. By the third month, she breached the 200K monthly mark. With many more good agents in tow, also generating handsome commissions within a short time, eyebrows began to rise.

Understandably, this was hitherto a general insurance outfit struggling to come to terms with the regular commissions' buildup on the Life business side. It had never occurred that tied agents could outpace permanent staff on take-home income.

What was even more shocking was the supposed ease with which these agents made sales and accumulated regular income. All the hard work was done in the field away from anyone at the head office.

What I had also done, was away from the knowledge of my general business colleagues. Before joining my team, the agents and especially those who had sold insurance products elsewhere wanted my assurances.

My agents wanted me to guarantee my administrative support at all times. Experiences elsewhere had made them run away from unsupportive bosses. My experience came to bear on this expectation.

Both the Chairman and the MD took note of the good performance and asked me to introduce my good agents to them so that they could thank and motivate them.

The chairman attended one of the early branch meetings so that he could express his satisfaction with the work done by the agents. This was a welcome relief to me.

The attention that my team was received caused discomfort in some quarters. Some permanent staff contemplated crossing over to the sales team because it was easier to make more money. This thinking was masked by the fact that I was in sync with my team, and experience made things look easy on the surface but deep down, I pushed hard for good performance.

Our agents quickly qualified for company facilitated car loans and the vehicles were in many instances better than what most permanent staff drove.

Colleagues, who had friends in other Life insurance companies, soon began to bring in conflicting reports. Some said that it was a good thing that we were getting noticed by the industry while others thought that there was something wrong with our products.

There were several attempts to water down the potency of the products.

The beauty of Life insurance products is that they must be sanctioned by the regulator and must have an actuary's certificate of approval. This was initially not known to the doubting Thomases. I had done everything by the book.

The doubts then shifted to the way information sat in the system. The actuaries came over to audit the information in the system and gave it a thumbs up.

Something wrong had to be found and, supporters had to be recruited into the bandwagon of the envious. On my end, the experience made me avoid trouble at work and all other places. I was now under the microscope.

All along, I knew that comparisons of take-home income across the divisions were not only unhealthy, but we were not comparing an apple for an apple. But here we were under one roof and one executive command.

One time, my very ambitious team managers, began to listen to the destructive voices and found resonance with people outside the business who could cause a punctured outlook on the Life business. To this end, efforts were made to have the product mis-sold then blame the same on the product structure.

The learning curve for the agents was very steep here. Soon those who mis- sold were terminated and their details submitted to the Association of Insurers. This locked them out of the industry permanently because any other company had to consult the central registry before onboarding agents.

On this account, the naïve agents lost their contracts on the advice of brave-cowards.

As our success soared high, so did our detractors work harder to cut us down to size. Soon the business began an upward trajectory that required more of the executive management's time. This was beside the very demanding nature of the general business book.

The Executive Management took the correct step at the time. They went out in search of an experienced General Manager level executive.

This gentleman took the reins of management from the General Manager who carried on with his duties in the general business side. Soon, a new structure was out. I continued to oversee business activities on both Individual and group life lines of business. We hired sales managers to run the branches. The underwriting department was beefed up and soon after, we took shape and commenced the actual journey to demerging the business from its composite form.

One of my pet projects was bancassurance. This was a novel idea back then. At the time, both the insurance and the banking acts discouraged entities on either side from partaking in the other's business.

It was an interesting time and we had models that allowed us to overcome the inconveniences of the acts without breaking any laws.

We embarked on a journey to work closely with the banking sector. We scored big with some top-tier banks and established good relationships with them.

Just as I was getting happy working with banks and managing the commercial aspects of Individual life and Group life, rifts started emerging in the business.

I had taken my annual leave and one of my sales managers found it timely to approach the executive management with allegations of my unfairness toward him by suppression. He presented copies of email correspondences to back up his claim. He went ahead and asked the team to get prepared for changes.

Upon my return from leave, the executive management sat me down and we were able to go point by point over the issues raised in my absence. It was found out that I was perfectly in order to have communicated the way I had done on email especially after all earlier correspondences came to light.

Despite my best attempts at getting out of trouble, a group of people within the organization had trained their eyes on a fragmented structure.

Not so long after, it was decided, that my Individual life business role should be hived off. I was left with the Group Life part of the business. Parting with a side that I had started from scratch was not a nice experience. Whoever thought of this, knew that it would not go down well with me.

I left to someone else the lovely products that I had developed and a strong team that had brought the company a sense of pride because a number of the agents were in the top 50 industrywide. By now, I was hardened and strengthened by my collective experiences.

So with a smile, I shook hands with the person taking over the individual side of the business. I had an appointment that afternoon with a broker and I used it to transition seamlessly into the new role.

The bond that I had built over time with the Individual life business agents was very strong. They kept coming back to me with complaints of this or the other and within a short time, cracks emerged in the team.

Most of their complaints centered on service and field support. The most that I could do for them was to urge the new management to help them out.

Ten years after these events, I caught up with some former colleagues and within no time, the conversations drifted to the good old days.

Some revelations that I would never have known of, came to the fore. My presence in the company from the word go, generated a challenge for some "blue-eyed" people.

References of how fast I was in setting up things got some people uncomfortable.

For me, I could clearly see that the General insurance business wheel could not turn in the exact same fashion as that of Life Insurance business. So whereas I was hitting all the right keys, the direct comparison made my approach rather unique from the norm.

What was at stake for me was much more than what was expected of other colleagues. I was racing against the clock of confirmation into permanent staff status. I also wanted to put to good use my experience and hence, I could not afford to turn at the same pace as everyone else.

My old colleagues also made it known to me that my move to Group life business, was because of my good contacts in the corporate world at the time.

Someone within the Division had gone to see a big client and was unable to close the deal. And when he narrated to us about his experience at the client's office, I offered to help.

The client knew me and quickly signed up for a sizeable group cover. This happened a few more times but it never dawned on me that it was frustrating someone within the division. This bit was not convincing at all for the role splitting.

One of my old colleagues, who now seemed to know what was happening at the time, threw in another angle to my change of duties.

It was also about lessening my role in Kenya so that I would find it attractive to go out into one of the subsidiaries across the borders to organize the business as I had done at home. It was about slowly but surely squeezing me into submission.

I now remembered that I had been loosely sounded out about going into one of the subsidiaries at the time, but I had such a young family then and it would create a strain on all of us. This revelation made me feel like the naïve rhino from our first story.

In retrospect, it may have been wise to go across the borders to help establish the business. For me, at the time, my discussions with colleagues seconded to the subsidiaries, only yielded lamentations about family and missed opportunities at home. These were enough for me to think otherwise.

One of my role models recently told me to always remember, that no business has "emotions" written anywhere in the strategy document. The exception is when describing the passion for customers. He went on "When this conflict arises between personal plans and corporate plans shape up or ship out."

Chapter 7

Transitioning into Banking.

After a decade in the insurance industry, it was time to move on. Again, a headhunter initiated a successful process that landed me in the banking industry. My bancassurance knowledge partly aided my move.

This was one of the rarest moves in banking at the time because an outsider moved in to occupy a senior role. I was employed as the Head of Consumer Banking.

I reported to the Group Managing Director and had responsibility for the branch network. We raised deposits to lend to our retail customers as well as those in the SME and Corporate segments.

This role also put me into the executive committee of management, the credit committee and the assets and Liabilities committee.

One of my new experiences was the rush by all and sundry to see me for loan facilities.

In the insurance world, I was always going after customers to favor me with their business.

In the banking world, it was the other way around. This came as a shock and at that point, I thought that things might be easier moving forward but we shall come back to this later.

I had to cool things off as I settled. I had to tell everyone, that I was still learning the ropes and it was prudent for them to see my colleagues for help.

The bank wanted to grow its branch network whilst solving prevalent problems within the existing branches. The bank had ambitions of strengthening its credentials by occupying a higher tier in the industry rankings.

This bank had positioned itself around the Small and Medium Enterprises space and was emerging very strongly as the preferred bank in its chosen segment.

The bank leadership had a solid team of very experienced people. It was a perfect blend of expatriates with global experiences gained in multinational banks, and an assembly of local talent that perfectly reflected the face of Kenya.

The management's composition was a reflection of the board and this gave us all a sense of security to commit long term. With an opportunity to participate in an employee share option plan in the works, there was no reason to look outwards anymore.

My first assignment was to figure out how to turn around the fortunes of Mombasa branch.

It was a favorite branch for all at the headquarters to visit because of its coastal location and its beauty.

This attraction notwithstanding, the branch was not carrying its weight as it was perennially below budget.

The branch had good potential but its problems went beyond the branch leadership team to the core of its offerings to the market.

The rigid old guards were quick to warn me about this branch. Many asked me to be careful because others had failed. The CEO was clear about closing it down if it did not turn around.

Something unique and drastic had to happen. We changed the management and then proceeded to introduce a new offering. My insurance industry background, help out a lot.

In my previous life, I had interacted with a SACCO based client in Mombasa for credit insurance. This group was very unique. It was formed by retirees from the Ports Authority.

Most of the members did not qualify for any loan products on account of advanced ages.

I knew that these SACCO members had a regular pension payment monthly and that they had all invested in other activities so that, the regular pension payout was free to service loan repayments.

We worked around all the risks involved and developed a product that suited these senior citizens.

I worked out an algorithm based Microsoft excel spreadsheet that when populated, one knew if the applicant qualified for a loan facility and also, the maximum amount that could go towards loan repayment.

The repayments were easy to manage because; we signed a check-off facility with the parent institution to favor us with the deductions. This was a common practice in the insurance sector.

From my end, this was the quick dividends of transmuting knowledge from one industry to another. It worked perfectly.

The default rate was near zero and credit insurance paid off any amounts resulting from customer deaths.

Mombasa branch's fortunes turned around. Everyone took note of this. The next assignment was the near simultaneous opening of new branches in Thika, Nakuru, Nanyuki and Eldoret upcountry, and Ngong Road, Muthaiga, and Gikomba in Nairobi. The existing branches underwent refurbishments to reflect the new SME look desired by the bank.

The consumer division was action-packed. This was so, on account of its numerous developments and, from the fact that it carried the bulk of the bank's employees.

At the end of my first year with the bank, we had met our targets. That year ended with a general election that in its wake emerged the worst ever politically instigated violence.

The protracted negotiations that ensued birthed a coalition government. In the embers of the restive atmosphere, a fractured nation took center stage and mistrust invaded the workplace.

The latent disdain toward each other's ethnic communities came to the fore and the tribal wounds inflicted by the skirmishes found fertile grounds in the office. I knew of this because branch staff started complaining about it.

These animosities became a diversionary smoke screen for what else was brewing in the background. There was a promise made to a senior executive at his employment interview. The structure was to accommodate an additional executive director from within the existing ranks.

A conversation with a past director of the board recently confirmed that a mention of the executive director position at a board meeting then, elicited mixed views.

The promoters of the discussions were firmly fixed on one of our colleagues but, the board had its reasons for deferring or rethinking the idea altogether.

The board threw in other options with comments like, "the finance division has a potential candidate, and so does the consumer division because they are meeting their targets."

That spanner in the works was to have serious ramifications.

Internally, it became obvious that what our boss wanted was an outright appointment of his preferred choice. So a plan was set in motion. First, the credit for any positive developments in my division was to be attributed to others.

Whenever a conspiracy needs feet, it finds them in willing members of your team, because, they stand to gain from the spoils of war. In this case, the promises of promotions were dangled in the way of my able deputies.

One of them was made to consistently fight me through an alliance of branch leaders and staff and the other was used to ferry information from our monthly branch heads meetings to the bosses.

By the time of briefing, the executive committee on the happenings in my area, whatever I was to report was already known and someone else already assigned credit for the effort.

So the credit of my efforts in Mombasa was assigned to the branch head there despite him not having the insurance knowledge to get the product off the ground. I had just recruited the branch head. Everyone else knew what had really happened.

The next item from the bag of tricks was a very bad eared rabbit. A proposal to dismantle my division was put on the conveyor belt. The idea behind these efforts was to create one commercial division with one head.

I was to be reassigned a customer service role and in the process, one obvious candidate for the directorship position would be left for board approval.

A strategic planning session was two weeks away and the board would retreat with management for three days. At my briefing on how to go about my presentation, I was asked to focus more on customer service elements. My instincts and passion guided me to add a slide at the end of my presentation.

I tabulated the big fixed deposit customers in categories commensurate with the size of their deposits and added my notes at the bottom.

At the presentation, I was able to demonstrate that we had very many customers who were also borrowing from us at the same time. I demonstrated that over time, there was the capacity to develop more products for our large customers.

These customers did not need just customer service but relationship management. There are other details that I choose not to print but all in all, the board got swayed to think my way.

The presentations were such that the directors were divided into two groups and management was to present to both groups. So we had to make the same presentation twice by moving from one room to the next.

The first group of directors was taken through a new structure and was told that the consumer division was not viable in its present form. The organizers were careful in making sure that I did not have a clue of the contents.

At the end of the retreat, the board reiterated the importance of the consumer division and asked the bosses to lend more support to it. I had survived but just for a while.

This did not go down well with the bosses and several readjustments to the plan were made and partly executed but, only for a short while.

Soon, it was year-end and it proved to be another good business year for my division.

A new thinking was happening at the board level. Initially, the bank was to be sold out to new owners but it seemed to take too long. Our employee share option plan promise was now thrown out of the window. Whoever wanted to buy the bank wanted a lean top as they thought that it was heavy at the time.

Within the space of nine months, all the executive committee members exited the organization. This included my bosses. One person was set against the other in a chain went on till everyone was out.

Only one person read the writing on the wall and exited before he was axed.

A lot was happening including someone in the Human Resources department having agendas to see to it that we exited quickly.

It was as if the board was saying that "you are either all in one team or, you are out of the bank."

This experience raises more questions than answers but lessons abound.

The term "smell the coffee," is often used to urge people to continuously scan the ecosystem for movements or changes that can affect them.

At higher levels of management, the coffee smells almost continuously but you cannot tell if it is being brewed for you or someone else. Things are complex and allies can easily turn into fierce enemies. This change of heart happens where competition for a scarce resource, is badly needed by someone.

Your performance dashboard indicators may be excellent on all fronts, but, without a plug-in to important but informal forums, you will always find yourself alone.

It later came to dawn on me that one of my deputies and a group of branch staff had regular cook-out sessions similar to the *korogas* at my third office automation company.

In the bank's case, these members of staff had the cook-outs invitation of someone high up the command and preferred a parallel way of getting information away from the official channels.

There was also another informal executive committee within the actual executive committee.

These informal forums served to shape up decisions before they were actualized in the official settings.

The instructions that I had wholeheartedly followed nearly seven years earlier, at the second insurance company, seemed to find a cousin in the presentations plan briefing session at the bank.

At the insurance company, I had been sent out to the branch with clear deliverables, to stifle an escalating go-slow. At the bank, I had instructions to "dance myself lame" then, limp into a lesser position and role; by presenting a diluted definition of my department.

With experience on my side, I took the lonely road that highlighted the actual situation. Oftentimes, you must take the correct road even if it leads to the possibility of consequences. This is what it means to be principled.

Principles are true all the time regardless of the sources of pressure.

Chapter 8.

The Second Bank

We dropped out of the first bank one-by-one at the executive committee level and it was now a case of "every man for himself, and, God for us all." Life had to move on.

After some months in the cold, I secured myself an opening at a bank of a similar size as my previous one. This move was one of redemption. In this market, a loss of a job in the banking sector invites condemnation and banishment from the industry.

Many people associate the loss of a job at the bank with theft but, ours was for different reasons.

Everything in this second bank was different. There was no executive position to perch me onto. I had to settle in for a relationship management role.

I moved from a corner office with hundreds of people under me, to a position where I had to do the actual work by myself. For my own record out there, the return to the industry brought me much needed relief. People who had refused to answer my phone calls now emerged from the blues with well-choreographed congratulatory messages. It is a bad thing to be jobless in Kenya because everyone thinks that you want to borrow money from them.

As I settled down to work in the corporate division, word filtered out to my former bank and as you know, people talk.

To some of my new colleagues, they were made to believe that, it was a matter of time before I got restored to a position similar to my previous one. This was never the plan but it certainly set some people in motion.

In any organization, there is always a succession plan, be it formal or imagined. Either way, there are vested interests that normally manifest through power games, information hoarding, mischief and outright confrontation.

My interest was to redeem myself and strategize on my next move. I actually had developed a genuine interest and plan into going it alone.

The script here was not any different from all the other places that I had worked in. I had invaded other peoples' space and plans as always were set in motion.

When you are battle hardened, you wisely choose your fights. I had chosen not to do battle in this bank and instead focus on my next life.

I used my short time at this bank to organize my business. All I wanted while at this institution was an opportunity to transition into my own business. Within a year, I was out this time around, on my own volition.

Chapter 9

The Switch from Corporate Life to Consulting.

At the time of exiting the bank, my first book "How to Undo Life's Airlocks." was ready for publishing.

I had been working my thoughts on the following questions that would prove powerful in my successive endeavors.

Why do people behave like brave-cowards?

How can these brave-cowards be helped out of their insecurities?

How can the other good employees be aided to overcome the presence and effects of brave-cowards?

These questions all pointed to working in the people and strategy space.

Armed with plenty of work-life experiences and the drive to get started on solving these three questions, I incorporated my consulting firm and got myself into the radar screens of all who cared to listen.

This part of the journey has lessons that I must share with you.

First and foremost, your status as a friend in everyone's list moves away from "a good friend" to that of an acquaintance. People befriend you mostly because of what you can do for them and seldom, what they can do for you.

This lesson came very early in my consulting pursuits. I found it easier to gain the trust and respect of people who had hardly experienced me in my previous work-life. My list of clients has continued on this trajectory.

For those who are close to you and, whose friendship with you is above your varying circumstances, this is the best time to know them.

Many others wait for you to collapse but when they realize that you have gone past the five to seven-year mark, they begin to show up with proposals.

The second lesson is that a consultancy with more experience is positioned better in the client's mind and eyes. Most people don't take chances and hence, your proposition must really be striking.

Your successes so far, are courtesy of your employers. In your past life, running successful campaigns, launching excellent products, successful management of teams, means little or nothing when you are too new in the consulting world.

The reality is that you must emerge from the shadows of your past work-life and, cut an image that can hold its own forte.

The second lesson has an exception for someone who pulls away from a bigger or existing consulting firm with a client or two. In this case, the trust already exists and the clients don't mind the change.

I found my third lesson when competing for business with another new consultant.

My competitor, had no clients but had just left working with a "big four" consultancy, and here contrary to my second lesson, experience gained while working for a big four consultancy, rubs off quite well when a smart guy goes it alone.

The two of us received a request to submit proposals for a strategic document proposal and thereafter to monitor the execution frequently.

It was an exciting opportunity for me because it would put me in a good place to answer and support the three questions that I wrote out earlier in this chapter.

After several long nights on the proposal, I submitted it and so did my competitor.

The management reviewed them both and after two weeks, the Managing Director of this medium-sized company gave me a thumb's up but still subject to the board's approval.

I began planning for the additional resources that would be necessary for successfully undertaking the assignment.

A week after the board meeting, my curiosity got me to phone the company. A dejected Managing Director answered the phone with the words, "you lost out." "How now?" was my response. As it transpired, my proposal was by far the better one.

The board of directors in their wisdom was uncomfortable with my experience. I was a banker and insurer at best with no consulting experience.

My competitor had what carried the day. The Managing Director was asked to find a way of getting my competitor to use my proposal. With an overbearing Chairman on his back, the Managing Director was overpowered in his efforts to merge two competing forces for the assignment. I lost out big time. In the consulting business, a good background is golden.

This meant for me, finding a place with the kind of respect that can easily rub off on me positively without killing my fledgling practice.

That opportunity came from the most unlikely quarters for me. I had never given it a thought but, the harsh realities of the consulting world moved me to this new epicenter.

My name got mentioned amongst others for a position at a famous Business School. This business school is part of a university that is famed for its excellence in all its pursuits.

This is the first time in the book, that I mention any of my previous employers by name. This was Strathmore Business School.

I got hired as Director of Executive Education and had the opportunity to do my consultancy work, provided, it never came in the way of my official duties. After a very exhaustive third lesson in my consulting journey, I found a place to mold me into a good consultant.

Strathmore Business School –SBS was many things in one. My business writing blossomed here when I became a regular contributor to the *Business Daily*, a newspaper widely read by top business executives.

SBS networked me with both Senior Executives who attended programs and, the faculty who proved to be perfect sounding boards on consultancy matters.

I got the chance to travel on assignments in Africa and Europe and learned from the best. The opportunities to work and network with senior government officials abound at SBS.

I have since my departure from SBS returned for a conference and a Director's program and will still do so again, whenever a chance avails itself.

As a consolation, the company that had denied me the opportunity to consult on strategy found the avenue to work with me on soft skills training. They have also benefited from my strategy services.

Top companies have also opened up for my services thanks to SBS.